Naaman
and the
Little Servant Girl

A true story from the Bible
With pictures by Graham Round

Winston Windows

This is a story from long ago,
eight hundred years before
Jesus was born.
God's people, the Israelites,
were at war with the Syrians.
The Israelites were often beaten,
but God always looked after them.

Naaman the Syrian was a very great general.

His army always beat the Israelites, God's people.

After one raid, Naaman captured a little Israelite girl and took her back to Syria to be his servant.

She had to wash the clothes and clean the house and cook the meals. It was hard work.

Naaman was very rich and famous.
He had lots of friends.

But one day, Naaman looked in the mirror
and had a terrible shock.

His face was covered with white blotches.

Every day the illness got worse.
Even the best doctor in Syria could not help him.

Soon people ran away when they saw Naaman. "I can never lead the army again," he said.

No one knew what to do—except for the little servant girl from Israel.

"God can make you better," she said. "Go to Israel and ask Elisha. He will tell you what to do."

So Naaman set off. He took his servants, and bags of gold and silver to pay Elisha the prophet.

It was a long, long journey from Syria to Israel but at last they came to Elisha's house.

Naaman knocked at the door, but no one came out to answer.

At last Elisha sent his servant with a message: "Go and wash in the River Jordan! Seven times!"

Naaman was very angry. "I haven't come all this way to wash in your filthy river!" he shouted.

But his servants said, "Sir, you ought to try. It might make you better."

"All right," said Naaman, "I will." So down he went to the River Jordan, and in he jumped...

SPERLOOSHHHHHH!!

"I'm better!" he shouted.
"The blotches have all gone!"

And Naaman ran all the way back to Elisha's house, to give him a thank-you present.

But Elisha would not take Naaman's present.
"It's God who has made you better, not me," he said.

Naaman could hardly believe it. The God of Israel loved even the enemies of his people.

When Naaman got back to Syria,
there was a big party.
And the first person to meet him
was the little servant girl.
"Hooray, hooray!" she shouted.
"I knew God would make you well.
He loves and cares for everyone
in the whole wide world."

You can find this story in your Bible,
in the Old Testament,
2 Kings chapter 5.